Ableton Live 5

P O W E R !

THE COMPREHENSIVE GUIDE

❋ ❋ ❋

Chad Carrier

THOMSON
━━━━━━✦━━━━━━ ™
COURSE TECHNOLOGY
Professional ■ Technical ■ Reference

Educational facilities, companies, and organizations interested in multiple copies or licensing of this book should contact the publisher for quantity discount information. Training manuals, CD-ROMs, and portions of this book are also available individually or can be tailored for specific needs.

ISBN: 1-59200-975-1

Library of Congress Catalog Card Number: 2005929809

Printed in United States

06 07 08 09 10 PH 10 9 8 7 6 5 4 3 2 1

THOMSON
™
COURSE TECHNOLOGY

Professional ■ Technical ■ Reference

Thomson Course Technology PTR, a division of Thomson Course Technology
25 Thomson Place
Boston, MA 02210
http://www.courseptr.com

Publisher and General Manager, Thomson Course Technology PTR:
Stacy L. Hiquet

Associate Director of Marketing:
Sarah O'Donnell

Manager of Editorial Services:
Heather Talbot

Marketing Manager:
Cathleen Snyder

Senior Editor and Acquisitions Editor:
Mark Garvey

Marketing Coordinator:
Jordan Casey

Project and Copy Editor:
Marta Justak

Technical Reviewer:
Adam Jay Southerland

Thomson Course Technology PTR Editorial Services Coordinator:
Elizabeth Furbish

Interior Layout Tech:
Digital Publishing Solutions

Cover Designer:
Mike Tanamachi

CD-ROM Producer:
Steve Albanese

CD-ROM Author:
Brian Jackson

CD-ROM Author of Resource ALP File:
Chad Carrier

Indexer:
Kelly Talbot

Proofreader:
Gene Redding

} Acknowledgments

Needless to say, I would not be where I am today without Live, both artistically and professionally. The program itself, and the fantastic people behind it, have opened doors for me that would normally have been impossible. I'd like to thank Gerhard Behles, Robert Henke, Dave Hill, Jr., Shawn Balm, Ulf Kaiser, Jan Bohl, Rutger de Groot, and Martin Froelich of Ableton AG for being so helpful and starting the momentum that has propelled my career forward. Special thanks to Friedemann Schautz of Ableton for converting this book's example files into their Live Pack format. I'd also like to thank Marta Justak of Course Technology for being such a terrific project editor on this book. Props to Adam Jay Southerland for providing his Technical Editing efforts—he caught many things I'd missed and helped work through the Mac/PC compatibility issues on the example files. Finally, my deepest appreciation goes out to my friends at M- Audio who have kept my brain sharp by asking me crazy questions about Live all day long—you guys really force me to think outside of the box.

On a personal note, I'd like to thank my grandmother, Helen, for taking care of me while I worked evening after evening on this book. Without her, I would have been too overwhelmed with the tasks of everyday life to get it all done—again. I'd also like to thank my parents, Jan and Mike, for their love, assistance, and support with my career.

Most of all, I'd like to thank you, the reader, for choosing this book in your quest for Live knowledge. I have strived to make it as easy to comprehend as possible while keeping the tone interesting and inspiring. I have filled its pages with nearly every morsel of information I could muster, yet I still think of new uses every day. I hope that my work takes the confusion out of Live and gives you the confidence and knowledge to create anything you wish.

About the Author

Chad Carrier

I've always had an affinity for music, even since early childhood, but I didn't learn to play an instrument until junior high. Before picking up the drums, my primary focus was computers. For years, the thought of using a computer to create music didn't even cross my mind—I was too immersed in the world of computer graphics and programming. Even through high school, as I progressed through marching and jazz bands, my musical knowledge didn't spill over into my computer endeavors.

Near the end of my junior year in high school, a friend laid a CD on me that changed my life: *Techno Mancer*. It was a collection of tracks from a Belgian record company, and it was also my first exposure to electronic dance music. It took everything I loved about rhythm and fused it with computer-whiz genius. I had finally found the perfect combination of music and computers. What I really loved was the sound—most of the drums were synthesized or sampled, which gave them a unique sonic texture. They were sounds I'd never achieve with a regular drum set.

Shortly thereafter, I sold my acoustic drums to purchase a set of electronic drums. Then came the sampler and the analog synths. Piece by piece, I began to amass a full MIDI production studio in the living room of my apartment. There I spent countless nights toiling away at my machines, digging into their depths and honing my technical skills. When it came time to gig, I'd move my entire studio to the venue, as I had no other means of performing the compositions. Oh, to have had Live in those days!

I moved to California to get into the music biz. For a while, I was an assistant engineer at a Hollywood studio. I quickly found, however, that the studio scene was not for me—it lacked the collective, creative atmosphere I assumed it would have. Because of my technical background, I got a job at M-Audio in their Technical Support department. As a support representative, I had to be familiar with all of the products, which included a small program called *Live*. I'd only been on the job a few months when version 3 came out, and Live started receiving some serious recognition.

During the 2004 Winter NAMM show in Anaheim, I had the great fortune of meeting the Ableton team, which included CEO Gerhard Behles and conceptualist Robert Henke, whom I knew from their musical project, Monolake. I also met Dave Hill, Jr., who had just been hired by Ableton and was the author of *Ableton Live 2 Power!* After watching me show off my knowledge of Live at the M-Audio booth over the four days of the show, Dave asked if I'd be willing to update his book for version 3. Of course I agreed.

By the time we started gearing up for the Live 3 update, Live 4 was starting to peek over the horizon. We discussed all the new features Ableton had in store and decided that updating the book to version 4 would be in the best interest for everyone, especially the readers. Therefore, when *Ableton Live 4 Power!* hit the shelves, it satisfied readers who were thirsty for two books instead of one.

I am now a Product Manager at M-Audio, responsible for designing DJ gear, controllers, and interfaces, all of which work with Live. I DJ and produce using Live, and I also provide private lessons on Live. And now that Ableton has released Live 5, it's time to update this book again. In other words, I eat, breathe, and sleep Ableton Live. Welcome to my world.

TABLE OF *f* Contents